Funeral and Mourning Traditions of the Old South

GOOD MOURNING!

Mitchel Whitington (signature)

Mitchel Whitington

ISBN 978-1-9393062-1-0

First Edition

Printed in the United States of America
Published by 23 House Publishing
SAN 299-8084
www.23house.com

Table of Contents

They shall not grow old,
as we that are left grow old.
Age shall not weary them,
nor the years condemn.
At the going down of the sun,
and in the morning,
We will remember them.

– Lawrence Binyon

Death in the Old South

In the Old South, grieving was as painful a process as it is today. The sorrow that they felt upon the loss of a loved one was severe, and to deal with it, they had many traditions for mourning and burial that were quite different from those of our modern day.

Funeral etiquette dictated to the genteel society of the South what was expected of them, and how they were to act, dress, and even go through the grieving process. There was an elaborate set of rules that governed behavior when a loved one passed into that final journey.

Compared to our world today, the funeral and mourning practices of the Old South might seem curious, if not downright morbid – as if they had some sort of strange fascination with the subject of death.

To paraphrase the great writer William Faulkner, "People took funerals seriously in those days. Not death; death was our constant familiar. Husbands and wives, uncles and aunts, all in their twenties and thirties and forties died at home then, in the same rooms and beds where they were born. But the funerals, the ritual ceremonial of interment, were tenuous yet steel-strong threads."

Exploring those "steel-strong threads" that Faulkner described can be fascinating, and occasionally, a little bizarre. Still, it is a subject that, once you cast your eyes on, is hard to look away from.

Welcome to the world of funeral and mourning traditions of the Old South, from covering the mirrors in a house where a death occurred, to the strange practice of sin eating. This array of oddities from the past has been assembled here for you to enjoy. A few will make you smile, others might bring a tear to your eye, and more than a few might send a shiver up your spine and make your skin crawl. If you are ready, and if you dare, turn the page and step into the funeral and mourning traditions of the Old South!

(overing /Mirrors

The movie *Fried Green Tomatoes* has a tear-jerking scene where the character of Ruth dies in her bed; surely there wasn't a dry eye in the theater at each showing. After Ruth's passing, her friend Sipsey quietly walks over and covers a mirror in the room with a cloth, and then stops the clock. Although there is no explanation for her actions, she was actually performing duties that were routinely done when a death occurred.

In the Old South when a person died, the mirrors in the home were covered immediately. Any cloth would work, but it was traditional to use black or white crape.

Some say that this goes back to Jewish tradition, others to the African-American culture, and still others trace it back to Europe. No matter what the case, there is no question that the covering of mirrors in a home of death was a widespread practice, from the poorest home to the richest mansion. In the book *Lincoln Memorial: The Journeys Of Abraham Lincoln*, author William T. Coggeshall wrote, "When Abraham Lincoln's body lay in state in the East Room of the White House, the windows at either end of the room were draped with black barege, the frames of the mirrors between the windows, as well as those over the marble mantles, being heavily draped with the same material. The heavy gildings of the frames were entirely enshrouded, while the plates of the mirrors were covered with white crape."

There are many reasons why people did this. One is the belief that when the spirit of a recently departed person left the body, it could take some time for it to cross over into the next life. Should the spirit glance into a mirror while it was lingering, it could become trapped in the world of the living instead of leaving for its new existence in the afterlife. In effect, it would stay and haunt the house.

Another reason given for covering mirrors is the belief that until the body had been buried, the next person to catch a glimpse of himself in a mirror would be the next to die. By covering the mirrors, it protected the people who were grieving at the house.

A much more practical reason, however, is that during a period of grieving a person was to focus on thoughts of the deceased, and not his own vanity. To that end, mirrors were covered so that during the grieving process people would not stop to adjust their clothing, comb their hair, or do anything that would detract from the loss.

Stopping the Clocks

If you tour some of the stately, old mansions of the South today, it's not unusual for the guide to point to a clock and – in whispered tones – say, "Back when the master of the house died in the year eighteen-whatever, the clock mysteriously stopped and has never ticked another second since."

The tour guide should probably be granted a bit of artistic license; while it was not common for clocks to stop when someone died, it was an ordinary practice to manually stop a clock at the time of death.

As with any old Southern custom, there are a number of possible explanations for this. The first is that the clock was halted as a courtesy to the people calling on the mourning family – without the clocks running, their visit would not be bound by time. The callers could stay as long as they liked without worrying about the hour.

Another possible reason is that the clocks were stopped out of respect for the family. Without the ticking and chiming, they would not be worried about the passage of time and daily responsibilities as they went through the grieving process.

Sometimes the clocks were stopped for the deceased, to allow the soul to move into the next life without worrying about human time. In fact, some believed that if the clocks continued to run before the funeral took place, the spirit of the deceased might get caught up in human time and remain in the house.

Yet another reason was simply superstitious – that if the clocks were not stopped, then bad luck would fall upon the members of the household. Of course, many areas of the Old South were steeped in superstition.

There is another reason that makes much more sense. When someone died in the old days, the family would have to send for the coroner, undertaker, doctor, or whatever person could pronounce and record the death. If the family home was out in the country, this process might take an hour or more. When the authoritative person arrived and the death certificate was being filled out, the time of death would be required, and it would be very easy to simply point to a clock that had been stopped at the moment of death for an accurate recording of the time.

Whatever the reason, it was highly unusual to hear the ticking of a clock in a home where a death had occurred in the Old South.

Turning Photographs

Although it was not as common as covering mirrors or stopping clocks, in some houses the portraits and photographs of people were removed, turned to face the wall, or placed face down on the table where they stood. In any of these cases, the images of the people would be hidden from view.

The main reason for doing this was out of respect for the mourning process; the family was supposed to dwell exclusively on their lost loved one and not think of other family members or friends.

Some historians have injected a bit of mirth into the explanation for this behavior, speculating that it was actually done to prevent a possible social faux pas. Prior to the funeral, there would be a parade of friends and relatives calling on the grieving family. If all of the pictures were on display, everyone would be able to see exactly who the family loved enough to have a picture of in their home... and who did not have that honor. This could cause hard feelings and disappointment, both of which were things that had no place in a house of mourning.

There was another, more interesting aspect to this practice, however. Some people believed that spirit of the departed one might wander about the house for some time before moving on to the next world, and if he saw the face of another family member or friend, he might beckon that person's spirit to join him in death... or worse, possess the unsuspecting person. As superstitious as this might sound, in many cases photographs were either turned to the wall or put face-down on tables to insure that the spirit of the departed did not attach itself to one of the living family members.

The photographs could be displayed again after the funeral, but until that time, the faces would be hidden from view.

Flowers on the Door

Even in our world today, an arrangement of flowers is placed on the door of a home that is grieving. This tradition goes back to the early days of the Old South, when black crape was put on the door to publicly announce that the house was in mourning. This is witnessed by the old verse: "Ring the bell softly, there's crape on the door."

In the olden days, black crape tied with ribbon was placed over the door, around the door facing, or upon the door knob or bell knob to inform a visitor that someone in the household had died. White ribbon was used for a child or young person, while black ribbon was used for someone older.

During a time of visitation, the door to the house was left ajar so that friends could enter quietly without having to knock or ring the bell, disturbing the mourners inside.

Over time, this practice gave way to a black wreath (also called a mourning wreath) on the front door. The circular wreath symbolized the circle of eternal life: one was born, they lived, they died, and then passed on to a new life.

This black wreath eventually gave way to a wreath of laurel, yew or boxwood tied with crape or black ribbons. Again, this was hung on the front door as a sign to passersby that a death had occurred in the house.

In modern days, colorful sprays of flowers are placed on the door of a home that has experienced a loss. It is done for much the same reason – to publicly announce that the family who lives there is in mourning.

A front door draped in black to show the house is in mourning

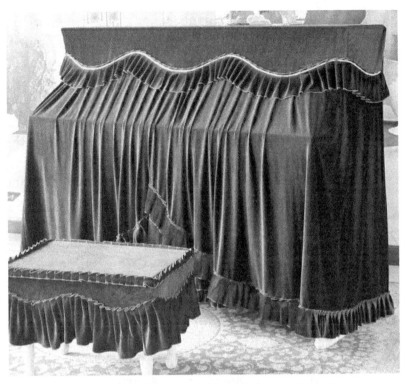

Closing the Piano

A piano was a staple in the parlors of many Old Southern homes, but after the death of a loved one, tradition dictated that it was completely closed up – both the lid that protects the strings and the key cover.

The sheet music was put away, and it was left looking abandoned. The basis for this is that in the world of Southern entertainment, the piano was a centerpiece. Daughters of the family were often trained in the piano, and they presented their skills at parties, recitals and other celebrations.

When friends came together for a small soirée, the piano was played as people gathered around to sing, or paired up in the parlor for the latest popular dance steps.

During the grieving period following a death, the family wanted to shun any appearance of gaiety, so the piano was closed and if there was a lock, that was engaged as well – there would be no music in the home while the family was in mourning. Some funeral homes even provided elaborate covers to further illustrate that the instrument was not to be played until the mourning period had ended.

In his book *Manners: Culture and Dress of the Best American Society* written by Richard A. Wells in 1894, the author writes against a long period of keeping the piano closed, saying, "Those who wish to show themselves strict observers of etiquette keep their houses in twilight seclusion and somber with mourning for a year, or more, allowing the piano to remain closed for the same length of time. But in this close observance of the letter of the law its spirit is lost entirely. The moment we begin to chafe against the requirements of etiquette, grow wearied of the darkened room, long for the open piano and look forward to the time when we may lay aside our mourning, from that moment we are slaves to a law which was originally made to serve us."

Wells was giving a nineteenth-century plea to mourn as long as you feel necessary, but once you feel like you're ready, put the mourning clothes aside and open up the piano!

Sin Eating

A meal prepared for the family of a departed one has been a long tradition in the South – one that is still carried forth to this day. There are few Southern folks who haven't experienced the palatial spread of fried chicken, mashed potatoes, green bean casseroles, and a myriad of other comfort dishes that are served to a family after the funeral.

Wakes have also traditionally included drinking as part of the celebration of the life of the one who has passed, with toasts to the dead, heartfelt remembrances, and warm wishes for the family.

None of these, however, are a part of one of the most bizarre death rituals that you're likely to hear about... the rite of sin eating.

This was certainly not a tradition that was practiced throughout the South; instead it was reportedly limited to certain cultures of the Appalachian Mountains in Alabama, Mississippi and Georgia. These people were very superstitious, and therefore clung to some of the fringe funeral traditions that had been brought over from Europe as America was settled. In the book *Death and Dying in Central Appalachia*, author James K. Crissman observed, "The Appalachians were not the elite or the aristocrats, but rather almost entirely unskilled or semiskilled workers who moved into the mountains to escape. Superstition has been a part of the Appalachian culture since the days of early settlement."

The practice of sin eating dates back to the United Kingdom. When a family member died, their loved ones would place a piece of bread and a drink (typically wine or beer) on the chest of the corpse or on the top of the casket. A designated person – a "sin eater" – was hired to come in and dine on the ceremonial meal, symbolically absorbing the sins of the departed and taking them onto himself. The belief was that the deceased could therefore present himself in heaven clean, pure, and free of sin.

In Welsh tradition, the sin eater not only took on the sins of the dead, but his action also guaranteed them rest in the afterlife – the spirit would not wander the Earth, which was a comfort to their family.

This practice perhaps got its start with the Biblical story told in Leviticus 16:8-10, where the Prophet Aaron takes two goats and sacrifices one to the Lord, and places the sins of the people on the other – the scapegoat – and sends it out into the wilderness. The goat took on the sins of the people, cleansing them.

14

In lieu of the goat of Biblical days, in this case a human would take on the sins... but not without a social stigma that followed the sin eater. He was an outcast from the church and from society, and often a loner that was summoned only for the heinous task of his chosen profession.

There would typically be only one sin eater per region, and upon his death, someone would step up to that position. As you can imagine, this was not a popular profession, and by the early twentieth century it had all but died out.

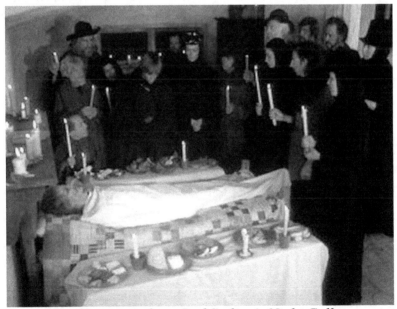

Sin eating scene from *Rod Serling's Night Gallery*

There have been several portrayals of sin eaters in current pop culture. In 1972, an episode of *Rod Serling's Night Gallery* showed a dramatization of the practice, and in the 2003 movie *The Order*, actor Heath Ledger enters into a battle with a modern day sin eater.

Sin eaters were often at odds with the church officials, since the practice was not one that was sanctioned by any form of organized religion.

Although those who took part in the ritual were usually part of the Christian faith, it actually went completely counter to the teachings of that faith. In Christianity, people were taught to seek forgiveness of sin only from God and that he was the only one who could provide such forgiveness. Sin eaters not only willingly took on additional sins – to the complete and utter disapproval of the church – but they also offered absolution to the person who had died through their own bizarre actions.

This long-lost funeral practice has faded into history, and perhaps deservedly so.

Feet First

You may have noticed that bodies are always transported feet first, whether it is a sick person on a hospital gurney, an injured person coming out of an ambulance, a coffin carried by pallbearers... or in the days long past, a dead body being removed from a home in the Old South.

As the legend from bygone days goes, a corpse was never moved head first because if the spirit of the deceased was still in the body, it would be looking back into the house as it was removed. The belief was that as this happened the spirit might beckon some other family member from inside the house to join him in death.

While that is a fascinating story, it is actually very natural for the feet to lead the body. We walk with our

17

feet, so it is symbolic that by moving a dead body feet first, it is moving toward its next destination in the next life.

Even in our world today, when we're in a car, our feet are in front of the body, so this continues to be something symbolic that translates to modern times.

There is a much more practical reason for moving a body feet first, however, and that is simply a balance of weight. The upper part of the body, the head and trunk, weigh much more than the legs and feet. This makes the body on a stretcher, on a gurney, or in a coffin easier to maneuver if transported feet first. If you've ever been in the hospital, you know that this is standard procedure when moving a patient.

People demonstrate this distribution-of-weight theory every day at the grocery store. If you consider a shopping cart, the back end is wider than the front end. This means that even if the cart is fully loaded, the front end will be lighter and is much easier to steer around corners and navigate through the maze of the food displays that always seem to dot the aisles.

Still, the idea of the deceased looking back into the home and beckoning someone to come with them is a much better story, and it was the origin of what turned out to be a very practical way of transporting a human body.

Mourning Periods

The Old South had strict mourning periods for proper society that came from tradition and were recorded in the etiquette books of the period.

When a woman lost her husband, she was expected to spend a full two-and-a-half years in mourning. The first part was known as heavy-mourning, which was followed by full-mourning, and then finally half-mourning.

Each of the stages dictated different types of dress and behavior. During heavy-mourning immediately following the death, a widow could only wear black clothing and simple jewelry. On the rare occasions when she left her home, her face was completely covered by a black veil. She could venture out only for specific events such as religious services and to attend other funerals, and then it was in the company of other women. Any social events were completely avoided. This was masterfully portrayed in the movie *Gone With the Wind*, when Scarlett O'Hara shocked all those present at the Confederate fund-raiser when she publicly danced with Rhett Butler.

The "shocking" dance scene from Gone With the Wind

After a sufficient time was spent in the heavy-mourning period, the widow would send out a formal card with a black border to friends and family announcing that her heavy-mourning had passed and that she could now receive visitors. This was the transition to full-mourning.

During full-mourning many of the rules of the previous stage still applied, however. The widow was expected to continue to wear black dresses and a veil, although she could accent her outfits with lighter cuffs and lace. Parties, weddings, public celebrations and other festivities were still forbidden to her.

During the final stage, half-mourning, the widow could change her wardrobe even more. Although she was still required to wear solid color dresses, she could now be seen in grays, purples, and other dark hues.

When the three stages of mourning had been completed, the widow was free to put away her grieving attire and return not only to her normal dress, but to all the functions of society as well. Some women got rid of their mourning clothes altogether, considering it bad luck to even have them in the house at all.

Mourning for a husband was by far the longest period that a lady had to endure. Children were mourned for a

21

year, parents for a year, and a brother or sister for only six months.

A gentleman had a much different mourning experience than his female counterpart. Because men were considered to be the bread-winners for the family, their mourning period was only three months. They wore dark suits with a black badge or rosette made of black fabric, and sometimes also wore a black armband or a black band on their hat.

Dressing the Dead

It is interesting that with so many rules regarding how those in mourning were supposed to dress, and for exactly how long, there were surprisingly few requirements for dressing the dead person in the casket.

Back at the turn of the century, in her book *Manners and Social Usage*, Mary Elizabeth Sherwood noted that when a man died he was usually buried "clad in his habit as he lived." In other words, he was buried in his usual suit ensemble.

Ms. Sherwood goes on to state, "For a woman, the wardrobe differs: a white robe and cap. For young persons and children white cashmere robes and flowers are always most appropriate."

So for a man, one of his normal black suits would be perfectly acceptable, but women and children were almost always buried in white, a symbol of the innocence of their soul.

And speaking of children, their mortality rate was much higher than it is today because of the terror of disease and the poor medical care that was available. For example, if a family had six children, it would not be unusual at all if only two or three of them made it to adolescence. Sadly, there were many funerals for the young in the Old South.

Children were dressed in white, but flowers were also often put in the casket surrounding the body as a symbol of life and beauty in the face of death.

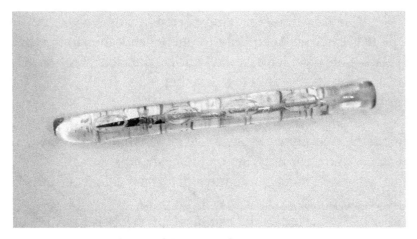

Tⲏe Tear Catcⲏer

There is one mourning item that traces its roots back to Biblical times, then to ancient Persia, to the Roman Empire, and finally into the Victorian Era. What is this item that survived from so long ago? A simple glass tube called the "tear catcher," or "lachrymatory." The latter name comes from the word lachrymose, which according to Merriam-Webster means "given to tears or weeping."

Tear catchers are small glass tubes that are often highly adorned. You will find them displayed in museums and old mansions throughout the American South, all with a story that, well, brings tears to the eyes.

As the tale goes, when a husband died, be it of disease, old age, or in the throes of the Civil War, the widow would take a small tube – approximately the size of a modern-day eye dropper – and as she cried, she would hold it to her cheek to catch the tears as they rolled down.

After her initial grieving period, a stopper was put in the tear catcher. According to one legend, the stopper had small holes which would allow the tears to slowly evaporate; when the tear catcher was finally dry, the grieving period was over.

Another version of the story was that the stopper was air tight, and after a year, the widow would open the tear catcher and pour the tears on the husband's grave.

As previously mentioned, tear catchers appear throughout history. There is a reference to collecting tears in a bottle in the Old Testament of the Bible, in Psalm 56:8-9, "Thou tellest my wanderings: put thou my tears into thy bottle: are they not in thy book? When I cry unto thee, then shall mine enemies turn back: this I know; for God is for me."

In ancient Persia, which is now Iran, a wealthy man could have any number of wives at the same time. Accounts from that period indicate that when such a man returned home from a long absence he would check each wife's tear catcher to see which one had cried the most while he was gone. One can only speculate that some of the tear catchers might have been filled at a fountain or spring when the wife learned that the man was returning home.

Tear catchers were also used in the mourning process in Ancient Rome. As ladies cried for the departed one, they filled their decorated glass lachrymatories and then placed them in the tomb with the body.

The Victorian Age brought a resurgence of the tear catcher among wealthy families, and in the style of the period, they were much more decorative and elaborate.

Apparently the tradition made its way into the grieving process of the Old South, for some tear catchers from the period have survived, whether they have been handed down through the generations of a family or made their way into a display case in a museum.

Given the difficulty in capturing each tear as it rolled down the cheek, most people in the modern world are probably relieved that this is a tradition that has faded into history and is not practiced today.

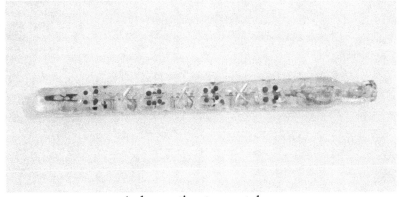

A decorative tear catcher

Mourning Jewelry

Mourning jewelry was generally worn by ladies who were grieving for a relative – a spouse, child, parent, or sibling. It was a connection to the deceased that would carry on long after the funeral was over and the loved one had been buried. Among mourning jewelry, broaches and pennants were probably the most common.

On occasion, men would wear mourning jewelry in the form of watch fobs or cufflinks, but this was a tradition that was usually reserved for women. In fact, during the first stage of mourning – called heavy-mourning – this was the only type of jewelry that a woman could wear.

During the preparation of the body, the undertaker would snip a lock of hair that would be given to relatives of the deceased, who would in turn incorporate it into a piece of jewelry designed for that purpose. Sometimes it was merely put into a pennant for display, while on other occasions it was woven into elaborate patterns.

"In Memory Of" broach with braided hair of the deceased

If long strands of hair were taken from the head of the body, more intricate items such as bracelets, necklaces, and rings could be woven for the bereaved.

A bracelet woven out of the hair of the departed one

If there was a photograph of the deceased, it could be incorporated into a broach that could be worn during the mourning period, as shown in the photograph below:

No matter what the form, mourning jewelry played a large part of the grieving process in the Old South, and many such items still exist today that have been handed down through the family generations.

Mourning Lithographs

When a loved one passed on, families conducted their expected mourning periods, but also looked for long-term ways to honor and commemorate the deceased. One such item that became popular in the nineteenth century was a "mourning lithograph."

The process of lithography was invented in Germany in 1796 by author and actor Alois Senefelder who was looking for an economic way to publish theatrical works. It turned out that his invention was also applicable to art, and prints could be produced at a much lower cost than ever before. The art world was changed forever.

One niche market for these prints arose rather quickly in the form of the mourning lithograph. In the above illustration, the graveyard scene complete with mourner would be printed, but the tombstone was blank. When a family wished to honor a departed one with a piece of artwork to hang in their home, the name and other information would be written on the tombstone, and the mourning art was complete and ready for framing.

Some were specialty items, like the print shown below that would be used for a soldier. Note the military formation in the background, and the weeping willow tree (a sign of mourning) over the grave. In this print, the name and other specifics are blank, waiting to be filled in.

THE SOLDIER'S MEMORIAL.

Even popular printmakers such as the firm of Currier & Ives produced mourning lithographs. This type of funeral art could be found in homes throughout the South.

Blank funeral lithograph, ready to be inscribed

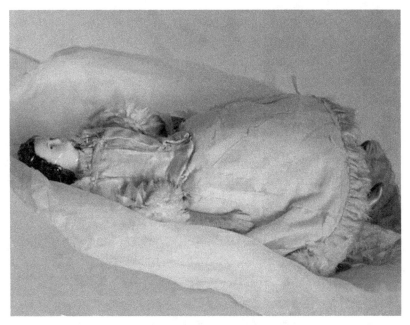

Grave Dolls

With the pain that always accompanied the loss of a loved one, families from the Old South were always looking for ways to preserve the memory of that person. Some took final photographs, others clipped locks of hair, but when a child passed a very unique tradition was sometimes practiced – the making of a grave doll, which were also known as effigy dolls or mourning dolls.

Even though the dolls were small, they were a faithful representation of the departed child. This was cost prohibitive for most families, but for those who had the means it was a unique, if not rather macabre, way to remember a child that had been claimed by death.

An artist who possessed the necessary skills would come and view and sketch the dead child, and then return to his studio where he would craft a likeness in wax. Sometimes the actual hair would be cut from the child's head to be used in the project as well.

The wax head would be attached to a body made of cloth and filed with sand. At that point the doll would be dressed in a representation of the child's clothes – sometimes made from a piece of the actual clothing – and hair from the deceased would be added to complete the effigy.

The treatment of the doll varied from family to family. Some put theirs on display in the home during the mourning period and beyond, while others actually left theirs on the grave after the funeral.

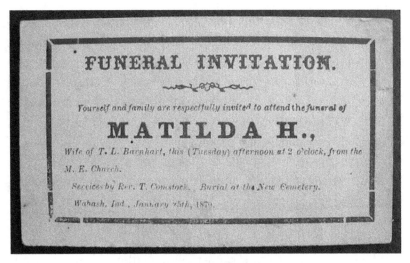

Funeral Tickets

Funeral tickets are one of the most interesting aspects of Old South memorial service traditions. In our world today, anyone can attend a funeral; you can even walk in to one where you don't know the deceased or anyone there. In the old days, however, it was customary to wait to receive a formal invitation to the service. These invitations – also called "funeral tickets" – were hand delivered to the people whose presence was desired. The ticket had to be presented at the door, and it was unthinkable for such an invitation to be ignored.

In some cities it was enough to put a death announcement in the newspaper and include the words, "friends invited – without further invitation," but the formality of an invitation was still used among the more elite society. Sometimes this was a necessity, because if the service was held in the home, seating would be very limited.

According to *Victoriana Magazine*, a funeral invitation would be engraved on small-sized note paper, with a black border, and would be worded in this manner:

"Yourself and family are respectfully invited to attend the funeral of Miss Stella Mason, from her late residence 123 Lang St. on Wednesday, July 14th, at 11 o'clock A.M. Burial at Forest Home Cemetery."

These were very stately and plain as compared to funeral tickets from the seventeenth and eighteenth centuries. The invitations from that period were usually wood engraved, and as morbid as it might seem, they were decorated with illustrations symbolizing death: hour-glasses, skeletons and bones, and Father Time and his scythe.

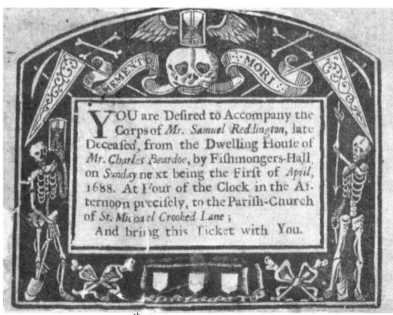

A 17th Century Funeral Ticket

For families that were not as well-to-do, the funeral home had a stock of invitations that had been printed with a heading such as "You are desired to accompany the Corpse of..." or "In Loving Memory of..." and the remaining details were filled in by hand before being delivered.

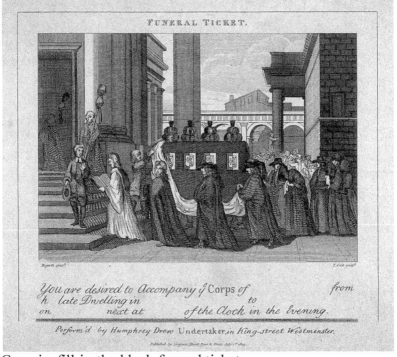

Generic, fill-in-the-blank funeral ticket

Pallbearers

As with today, the pallbearers of the Old South had a dual purpose: the physical transportation of the casket from the house (or funeral home) to the place of service, and then to the cemetery; and to act as an honor guard for the person who had passed. The pallbearers would walk solemnly behind the horse-drawn funeral wagon, or have their own carriage.

Six to eight men were chosen from the friends and relatives of the deceased, and were sent written requests for their services. Badges or ribbons were pinned to the lapels to denote their position at the funeral. Women were not allowed to be pallbearers, since presumably they would not only be consumed with grief, but would not have the strength necessary to lift the wooden coffin.

The pallbearers in the Old South wore black gloves when attending an elderly person, but white gloves for a young person. Gloves were always worn, however, because of the widespread belief that touching an occupied casket could allow the spirit of the deceased to enter the pallbearer's body.

The name comes from the term "pall," which is a heavy cloth that was used to drape the coffin. The men who carried the pall-covered casket therefore became known as "pallbearers."

An exception to the man-only tradition occurred when a young girl passed. In that case, friends that were her age could be asked to serve in the capacity, as shown below:

Flowers at the Funeral

Who hasn't picked up the phone and ordered a spray of flowers upon hearing of a death from someone in the community? Throughout the ages flowers have been an integral part of a funeral, and they certainly make the service beautiful. The original reason was for a much different reason, though, and certainly out of necessity – the sweet aroma that they produced would help mask the odor of body decomposition.

The first instance of flowers being used in such a manner goes back goes back almost fourteen thousand years ago – that is about 12,000 B.C. This was proven because graves from the Natufian period were discovered in Raqefet Cave in Mt. Carmel in northern Israel where dozens of impressions of Salvia plants and other species of sedges and mints were found under human skeletons. Clearly, this practice has been around for a while.

The Greeks, Romans, Egyptians, Israelites and numerous other cultures used frankincense and myrrh as part of their burial preparations in order to cover the odor of the dead body in much the same way.

In 1874 a famous example of the use of funeral flowers happened at the funeral of President Andrew Johnson, who succeeded Lincoln after the infamous assassination at Ford's Theatre. Just as an aside, Johnson was the first President to ever be impeached, and is generally regarded as one of one of the worst presidents in history.

Johnson died on July 31, 1875, and his funeral was held several days later on August 3 in Greenville, Tennessee. Embalming was just starting to be done in America during the Civil War, but it was not that common. Johnson's body had therefore not been embalmed and was starting to smell terrible in the summer heat.

As the story goes, mortician Lazarus C. Shepard closed the casket and piled fragrant flowers on top and around it – the sweet fragrance of the flowers hid the smell of decay long enough for the funeral to take place.

As embalming became more widespread, the need for masking unpleasant odors waned, but the tradition of providing flowers had become a mainstay for funerals and therefore continued.

The practice continued with what funeral historians call the "In the Garden" movement. In 1914, the musician C. Austin Miles composed the famous funeral hymn *In the Garden*.

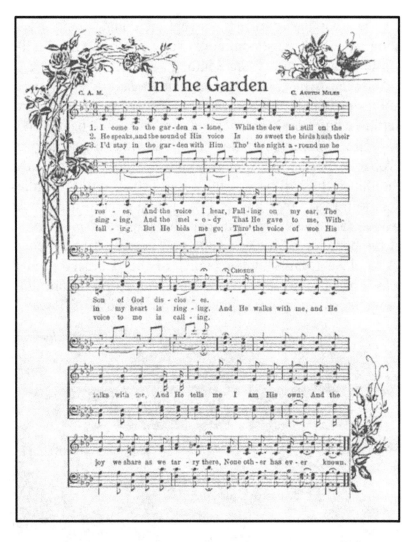

As the song goes, "I come to the garden alone, while the dew is still on the roses. And the voice I hear, falling on my ear, the Son of God discloses. And He walks with me, and He talks with me, and He tells me that I am His own; and the joy we share as we tarry there, none other has ever known."

47

The popularity of hymn swept the country, and it was soon one of the most commonly sung funeral hymns in the United States, not just the South.

Because of this, a movement began where funeral homes presented the bodies of the deceased in a "garden" setting using floral arrangements and a painted backdrop.

The importance of flowers in the funeral service was probably best shown by the role of the flower lady. Similar to the pall bearer, the duty of the six flower ladies was to transfer the flowers from the funeral to the flower wagon, and then arranged them for the graveside service at the cemetery. Much like the pall bearers, flower ladies were close friends of the family of the deceased, and it was a great honor to be chosen. It was an important duty as well, especially considering the original use of flowers.

Funeral Biscuits

This is an Old South tradition that sounds a little stranger than it actually is. Funeral biscuits – which were also called burial biscuits or funeral cakes – were simply cookies that were given out at the end of the service to the mourners, or sent to people who were not able to attend. They were often wrapped in paper that had the deceased's name, Bible verses, or even poems as shown in the photograph above.

According to the book *Funeral Festivals in America* by Jacqueline S. Thursby, "...a prevailing funeral custom was that a young man and young woman would stand on either side of a path that led from the church house to the cemetery. The young woman held a tray of funeral biscuits and sweet cakes; the young man carried a tray of spirits and a cup. As mourners passed by, they received a sweet from the maiden and a sip of spirits from the cup furnished by the young man. A secular communion of sorts, these were ritual behaviors that transcended countries of origin and melded a diverse young nation with the common cords of death, mourning, and tradition. The funeral biscuit served as part of a code representing understood messages of mourning, honor, and remembrance."

This practice was brought over from Europe, where it was widespread. In England and Wales sponge cake-like biscuits were used, and a dark chocolate cake was served at funerals in Belgium.

Other areas of the world had similar traditions; in Jamaica, a sweet corn cake was placed into the coffin of the deceased to provide nourishment for their journey to the other side. These were known as "Journey Cakes."

But how did the practice get started in Europe? Some anthropologists believe that the origins trace all the way back to a grisly practice of early man, where small pieces of the dead were eaten just before burial in the hopes that part of their essence would be transferred to the living.

As humans became more civilized, this ghastly ritual could have morphed into the consumption of food for a similar purpose. For example, in Germany, "corpse cakes" were eaten to symbolize eating the dead. When someone died and the corpse had been washed and put in the coffin, a female relative would prepare leavened dough and put it on a piece of linen on the body's chest. It was believed that as the dough would rise, it would take on the virtues of the deceased. The dough would be baked into cookies or cakes, and the essence of the dead one would therefore be passed on to the mourners who ate the corpse cakes.

In Hungary and other parts of Europe, a meal was placed beside the corpse for an hour for the same reason – the belief was that it would absorb the qualities of the dead person. The mourners would eat the meal and then take these on.

A similar practice in Ireland involved tobacco – a bowl of snuff was placed on the deceased's chest or on the coffin, and as mourners passed by they each took a pinch.

From these various traditions it seems certain that the practice of serving funeral biscuits was handed down from European ancestry to the people of the Old South. But as with most things in their lives, the tradition was handled in a genteel manner.

It is a practice that has disappeared from modern day funerals, but in the spirit of the old tradition, a recipe for funeral biscuits follows:

Funeral Biscuits

Ingredients:
1 cup butter
¾ cup sugar
½ cup molasses
1 egg
2½ cups flour
1 teaspoon baking soda
2 teaspoons ginger

Instructions:

After blending the butter and sugar, stir in the molasses and the egg. Continue by mixing in each of the dry ingredients in order.

Roll out the dough onto a floured sheet of wax paper, cut into circular cookies, and bake in a 350 degree oven for 10 to 12 minutes.

Holding a Button

In the bygone days, if you were in the street and a funeral procession happened to come by, you would immediately grab a button on your coat, your collar, or some other piece of clothing and hold onto it tightly until the procession was out of sight. The superstitious belief was that a person had to do this to keep death from coming after him.

The basis for this was the notion that seeing the funeral procession connected the person to the dead, but the button would connect him back to the living.

Different areas of the South had variations on this, however. A similar belief was that a person should touch their collar and hold it until the hearse passed. Still another version dictated a touching of the nose after the collar to avoid having a hearse come for you.

Several children's poems contained the specific rules for encountering a funeral procession. One such rhyme was:

Touch your collar,
never swallow.
Touch your collar,
touch your nose,
never go in one of those.

Tђe Fuɲeral Proᴄessioɲ

Like everything else associated with death in the Old South, the funeral procession was dictated and regimented, although there were variations that depended on the number of carriages used... which was directly proportional to the amount of money that the family was able to spend.

The hearse led the procession; it was an elaborate black carriage with glass windows on all sides so that the coffin and the flowers that were inside could be viewed. A number of black horses drew the hearse – the more horses, the greater the expense. The corners of the carriage could be embellished with ostrich plumes, as well as the heads of all the horses… also at an additional cost.

The first carriage to follow the hearse was reserved for the clergy and the pallbearers. If this luxury was not affordable for the family, then the pallbearers would simply walk behind the hearse.

The next carriage transported the immediate family, followed by another with the extended family, and finally the distant relatives and friends.

If the dead person was a military officer, a horse in full regalia and draped in mourning would follow the hearse. Also, if the deceased was part of a Masonic organization then variations specific to that group would be interjected into the proceedings.

Once the procession was assembled, it would proceed at a slow, walking pace to the cemetery. If the deceased was an important person, sometimes the route was altered to go through the more upscale parts of town to make a better showing.

On the other hand, if carriages could not be afforded for everyone, the mourners would follow the hearse on foot to the cemetery.

Sitting Up with the Dead

There is perhaps no tradition that is more heavily steeped in Old South mourning practices than sitting up with the dead. It has been done throughout the memorable history of the country.

Like many other funeral and mourning traditions, it has its roots in practical application, as morbid as they might be. Prior to embalming becoming widespread, the smell of the decaying body would attract rodents, so a family member was always stationed beside the body to keep any would-be predators away.

Another reason was the fact that on rare occasions people who were considered to be dead were only in a coma, and showed signs of life before the actual burial. Again, this was rare, but one of the responsibilities of a family member tending the dead was to watch for a breath, a movement of a finger, or a tear tracing down the face from the eye.

As the medical world became more precise and embalming more common, those reasons faded. Sitting up with the dead became more of a symbolic, respectful thing. Family members and friends would take shifts sitting beside the body until the funeral and interment.

This practice has continued from the Old South through current day, and a few years ago the country singer Ray Stephens even recorded a song about it…

From "Sittin' Up with the Dead"
by Ray Stephens

Well out in the country we didn't have mortuaries
and so it was always customary
For the undertaker to do his job
and lay your kin out there at home.

Well the church would loan ya foldin' chairs
and you'd have visitation and everything right there
and when the nighttime come you had to sit up with the dead
'cause it wasn't right to leave them alone…

The act of sitting up with the dead should not be confused with the Jewish custom of sitting shiva, where the relatives gather in the home of the deceased and receive visitors during a seven-day period of mourning, which begins immediately after burial.

Facing East

A visitor to cemeteries in the Old South will notice that the graves traditionally face toward the east. As one might expect, this is not a random coincidence.

This practice actually comes from the Christian tradition of burying a body with the head to the west and the feet to the east – this would mean that the body itself would be facing toward the easterly direction.

On some occasions when the traditional east-west positioning could not be used for a grave, the body would then be buried in a north-south orientation, on its side, facing east.

The basis for this burial procedure can be found in the Bible, Matthew 24:27, which says: "For as the lightning cometh out of the east, and shineth even unto the west; so shall also the coming of the Son of man be."

In other words, when Christ returns to earth, he will appear from the east, and the bodies are positioned to witness the Second Coming.

Ezekiel 43:1-2 says: "Then the man brought me to the gate facing east, and I saw the glory of the God of Israel coming from the east. His voice was like the roar of rushing waters, and the land was radiant with his glory."

Again, the glory of God was coming from the east, which was another reason to face bodies in that direction.

A benefit of this positioning is that when the sun rises in the eastern sky every morning, it shines onto the graves of the beloved departed.

In certain Christian denominations, members of the clergy are buried in the opposite direction among their parishioners, their bodies facing the west. This is done so that when the Second Coming occurs, the clergy will rise facing the members of their congregation, and they will be prepared to minister to them.

The burial toward the east predates the Old South, though, and has almost always been done for religious reasons. According to author William Tyler Olcott in his 1914 book *Sun Lore of All Ages*, the ancient Egyptians built their temples facing towards the East, as did the ancient Greeks, so that they would face the rising sun every day.

The Yumanas of South America buried their dead in a sitting position facing east, which was the abode of their supreme deity, who would one day take unto himself all true believers.

Medieval Russian Tartars placed statues facing eastward in mounds over their graves, and the legendary

Solomon's Temple in Jerusalem was open to the east, and closed to the west.

Clearly graves facing east have been the norm for many years gone by, through the period of the Old South, and even into today's world.

Older cemeteries may not actually face due east, however. Even though compasses existed since around the year 1000, they weren't always common and available. Cemeteries therefore had to rely on using the rising sun as a guide. Still, the intent is there, and today one will find that most Southern graves face the east.

Grave Houses

It was customary in some areas of the Old South to build a shelter over a grave, or set of family graves. These interesting little structures were known as grave houses.

Some were rudimentary structures make of logs or clapboard, while others were sturdier and were constructed of rock or brick. No matter what the material, the design was very similar across the South. The small houses had corner posts, a roof, and a fence around the base. Most had gates to allow the family to visit the graves to place flowers and pay respects. Still others had full walls that completely enclosed the grave.

The main reason given for the grave houses was to protect the grave from the weather and therefore excessive settling, and keep the rain off of the face of the deceased.

The grave house performed many different functions. One was to protect the grave from desecration by animals in rural cemeteries, or in the case where the cemetery was in an open field, to keep grazing cattle from knocking over the tombstones. The grave houses also helped to make graving robbing more difficult – something that was a problem in those days.

A more spiritual explanation was that the houses represented the mansion that the departed one would have in heaven, as Jesus himself described in John 14:2 – "In my Father's house are many mansions: if it were not so, I would have told you. I go to prepare a place for you."

Although the building of grave houses is no longer practiced, these structures can still be seen in a number of cemeteries throughout the South.

A Grave House in Crenshaw County, Alabama

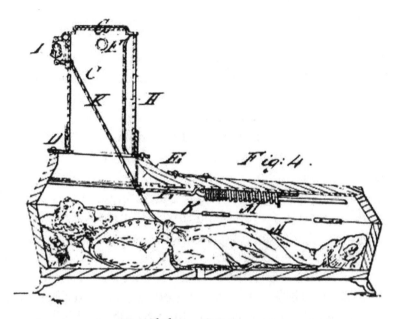

Coffin Alarms

A major fear in the 1800s was that of being buried alive. Thanks to cholera and yellow fever epidemics and questionable medical care, the 19th century saw a number of cases of premature burial. Because of this, there were many patents filed for "coffin alarms" that would provide a means for someone who had suffered such a fate to notify the above-ground living that they were in need of assistance.

It was such a widespread fear that Mary Todd Lincoln, the wife of the President, wrote down her wishes: "I desire that my body shall remain for two days with the lid not screwed down."

A Dr. Johann Gottfried Taberger from Germany designed a coffin that included a system of ropes that were attached to the corpse's hands, feet and head, and led to an above-ground bell. The theory was that should a person wake up after the burial, their movements in the coffin would ring the bell and provide an alert. Unfortunately, this was a miserable failure. What Dr. Gottfried didn't anticipate was that as the corpse began to decompose, it bloated and swelled, causing it to shift inside the coffin – all movements that would ring the alarm bell, and have people running to the cemetery with their shovels.

American doctor Timothy Clark Smith was so afraid of falling into a coma and being buried alive that he designed a grave that had a cement tube with a glass cover that started above ground, and ended up in his coffin above his head. When he died – interestingly enough on Halloween, 1893 – he was buried as he prescribed. The curious would peer down the tube to look at his head for any signs of life, but none were ever observed, and the good doctor's body lay in silent repose. Unfortunately, as the years went by people could continue to look into the tube, where they would see Dr. Smith's decomposing head. His grave is still there today, but thankfully condensation blocks any view of the head.

This fear of being buried alive wasn't constrained to the Old South. Around the turn of the 18th century, Duke Ferdinand of Brunswick had a coffin built that included a window to allow light in, and a tube to provide a fresh supply of air. He was going to be laid to rest in a mausoleum, so when the coffin was placed on its shelf, the lid would be locked, as would the door to the mausoleum. Two keys were safely tucked away into his burial shroud, however: one for the coffin, and one for the door to the mausoleum. As it turns out, Duke Ferdinand didn't have to use either one.

Advertisement for a coffin with alarms

In 1885, Charles Sieber and Frederick Borntraeger of Waterloo, Illinois received a patent for a "grave signal for people buried in a trance." It contained a standard bell alarm and a pop-up flag by the tombstone that was activated by a string attached to the finger of the deceased. It further included a fan housing to blow air into the coffin if activated, and a viewing tube with a window and lamp to examine the corpse.

An entire book could be written containing all of the patents that were granted in the 1800s to address the issue of premature burial, but oddly enough, there are few if any legitimate cases of a person being rescued from the grave after interment.

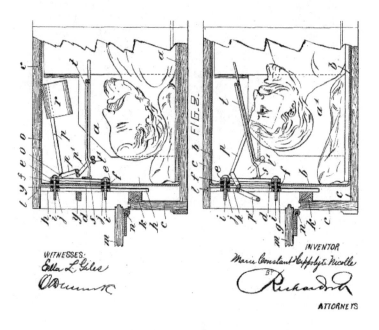

All of these things may seem to be a bit extreme in our world today, but safety coffins are still manufactured.

Inventor Fabrizio Caselli came up with a coffin in 1995 that included an emergency alarm, two-way intercom, a flashlight, oxygen tank, heartbeat sensor and heart stimulator. It may be that the fear of being buried alive is alive and well in our society today.

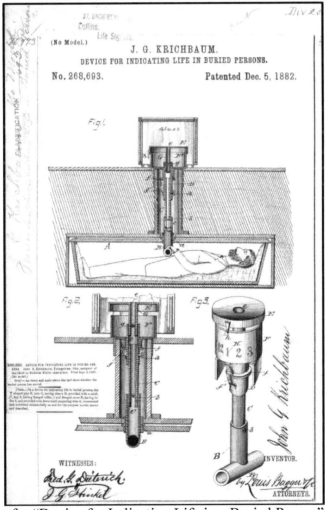

Patent for "Device for Indicating Life in a Buried Person"

Resurrection Men

When the funeral was over and the family had departed the cemetery to continue their grieving process, a threat to the body of their loved one was lurking in the shadows… the Resurrection Men.

This colorful moniker was simply another name for the people involved with the dastardly practice of body snatching, or grave robbing. The men usually worked in small groups and would regularly scout a cemetery for any sign of an upcoming funeral. When they saw a fresh grave being dug, it was a simple matter to wait until the burial was held and darkness fell.

Fresh graves were preferred for two reasons. First of all, the loosely packed dirt made the coffin easier to disinter; and just as important, fresh bodies brought higher prices.

71

As wicked as this practice was, the customers for the pillaged bodies were respectable doctors and medical students. They needed cadavers to dissect to both learn and further their craft, and these were unfortunately in short supply... so they turned to the resurrection men.

The entire practice was a double-edged sword of morality. Without the cadavers, medical science could not have continued to advance, and doctors could not have honed their skills to help their living patients. On the other hand, the crushing blow to a grieving family when they returned to the cemetery to see that their loved one's grave had been plundered would be unimaginable.

As medical schools were established, however, the need for bodies continued to grow, and the law of supply and demand kept the Resurrection Men in business.

Woodcarving of Resurrection Men at work

Sometimes authorities caught the thieves in the act, and on occasion even charged a doctor who was using a purloined cadaver for research. For example, Dr. Charles Knowlton was imprisoned for two months for "illegal dissection" in 1824, a couple of months after graduating with distinction from Dartmouth Medical School. The doctoral thesis that he had written in school defended dissection on the basis that "value of any art or science should be determined by the tendency it has to increase the happiness, or to diminish the misery, of mankind." Knowlton called for doctors to help solve the cadaver shortage by donating their own bodies for dissection in their wills.

The Resurrection Men were not only a very real threat, but they were greatly feared by the families of those who had just lost a loved one. Stories such as Robert Louis Stevenson's *The Body Snatcher* only fueled these fears. Stevenson wrote about the body of a proper lady being stolen from the graveyard: "The wife of a farmer, a woman who had lived for sixty years, and been known for nothing but good butter and a godly conversation, was to be rooted from her grave at midnight and carried, dead and naked, to that far-away city that she had always honoured with her Sunday best; the place beside her family was to be empty till the crack of doom; her innocent and almost venerable members to be exposed to that last curiosity of the anatomist." That was enough to make any living person cringe, especially those who had just lost a loved one.

The Resurrection Men therefore endeavored to hide their work, not from a viewpoint of protecting the grieving family, but instead out of self-preservation. If a cemetery was being pillaged of newly-buried bodies, an uproar of the local citizens would call for measures to be put in place to apprehend the culprits. In other words, it was simply better for business if no one knew that a body had been stolen.

To that end, the grave robbers would spread out a canvas for the dirt to be shoveled onto as they dug. After removing the body, the coffin was closed back and the dirt carefully replaced. Any flowers or other adornments were put back like they had originally been placed, and the men were off into the night to deliver the body.

A safer form of body snatching was also employed by Resurrection Men; they would hire women to portray grieving widows and claim the bodies of men who died in poorhouses. Since most men had no known relatives, or even certain identities, it was a relief to the authorities when a "relative" showed up to take the body.

A mortsafe to foil the Resurrection Men

Because this thievery was so widespread, steps were taken to protect new interments. Some cemeteries hired guards to stand watch at night, and in some cases families had an iron cage called a "mortsafe" installed over the grave to prevent it from being re-opened.

Still other inventions such as Grave Guns and Coffin Torpedoes (which will be discussed in following chapters) took a more aggressive approach to stopping the Resurrection Men. Unfortunately, the problem never completely went away.

Coffin Collars

A passive defense against the Resurrection Men was a device known as a "coffin collar." Its sole purpose was to keep the grave robbers from removing the body, and it actually worked quite well.

The mortician would place an iron collar around the neck of the deceased, and bolt that to the bottom of the coffin. The death clothes would be arranged to hide the iron collar, and no one would be the wiser.

Should the Resurrection Men come calling at the grave, however, when they tried to remove the body, they would find that it was securely fastened to the coffin. Unblemished whole bodies were required by the medical world, so the grave robbers could not do any dismemberment. That left them the options of either removing the entire coffin from the grave and unbolting the metal collar – which would take time and leave visible evidence of their work after the fact – or abandoning that particular grave. The latter, of course, was what the family of the departed was hoping for when they employed the use of a coffin collar.

The following photograph shows the bottom of the collar as it would be bolted into the wood of the casket.

This was a simple and inexpensive, yet effective, method for protecting the body of a loved one after interment.

Grave Guns

A more aggressive form of defense against the Resurrection Men was a device known as a "grave gun." It was mounted on a swivel and placed at the foot of or on one of the corners of the cemetery plot.

Trip wires were positioned around the perimeter so that if anyone disturbed the grave, the gun would swing around and fire, killing the interloper.

There were a number of problems with grave guns; the first was that the Resurrection Men would send women dressed in black into the cemetery after the funeral, posing as a mourner, but instead the "grieving woman" was there to scope out the placement of the trip wires and grave guns. These spies would then report back to the exact locations of the devices, and the grave robbers could disable the traps and go on with their terrible business.

The other problem is that on occasion, an innocent person would hit the trip wire and set off the gun. This led some cities to ban the use of grave guns altogether, while others stipulated that the guns be loaded only with a wounding shot, not a lethal load.

Signs such as the one at the first of this chapter were also required to let people know that grave guns, also called "spring guns" because of their pivoting mechanism, were in use in the cemetery.

Grave guns and all the trappings were expensive, so families often rented the entire apparatus for the period when the body would be fresh and a commodity for the Resurrection Men – usually only a few weeks.

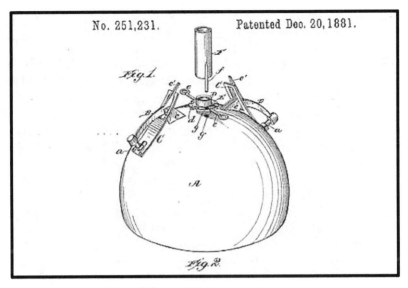

Coffin Torpedoes

Perhaps the most effective of the methods used against the Resurrection Men were Coffin Torpedoes. These devices were interred with the bodies – some actually inside the coffin, some beside it, others on top of the lid. A number of different patents were granted over the years for different devices. All had the same purpose, though... to explode should anyone disturb the grave.

The Coffin Torpedo was armed after the funeral was over and the family left the cemetery, and if the grave was left undisturbed, no one would even know that it was there. If the Resurrection Men came to visit, however, they were in for a deadly surprise.

An inventor and artist named Philip K. Clover from Columbus, Ohio patented a coffin torpedo in 1878. His "torpedo" was basically a small shotgun fastened to the inside of the coffin, with a tripwire attached to the lid. If someone tried to open the coffin, the torpedo would fire out a lethal blast of lead balls in a scatter pattern much like a shotgun – no matter where the Resurrection Men were standing around the grave, they would be hit.

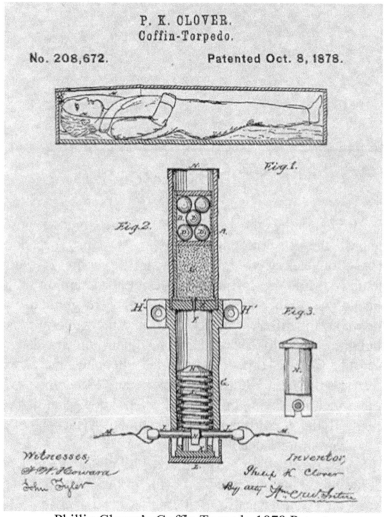

Phillip Clover's Coffin Torpedo 1878 Patent

An advertisement for another Coffin Torpedo read: "Sleep well sweet angel, let no fears of ghouls disturb thy rest, for above thy shrouded form lies a torpedo, ready to make minced meat of anyone who attempts to convey you to the pickling vat." Certainly a little macabre, but it does get the point across.

The torpedoes were arguably very successful. Consider the following newspaper story:

GOOD FOR 'EM.

One Ghoul Killed and Another Wounded While Robbing a Grave.

Mount Vernon, O., Jan. 19.—It is reported from Gann, a small town in this county, that while three grave robbers were violating a grave in the cemetery there, a torpedo which had been placed on top of the coffin for protection, exploded, killing one of the ghouls and wounding another.

It reads: "Good For 'Em. One Ghoul Killed and Another Wounded While Robbing a Grave. Mount Vernon, Jan. 19 – It is reported from Gann, a small town in this county, that while three grave robbers were violating a grave in the cemetery there, a torpedo which had been placed on top of the coffin for protection, exploded, killing one of the ghouls and wounding another.

The Resurrection Men had no way of telling whether a grave had a torpedo or not, so it would definitely give them pause in their occupation.

Headstone Images

When it was time to erect a memorial marker at the grave of a family's dear departed one, the image and artwork carved into the cemetery headstone was not only beautiful, but meaningful as well.

Some symbols were chosen to commemorate the occupation of the deceased, or a fraternal organization that he or she belonged to. Still other icons were carved into the headstone to represent the family's mourning, or the dead one's assent into heaven.

There are many different symbols, and they can be found in graveyards throughout the South. Some of the most popular ones are presented here with an interpretation of their meaning to aid as you begin to explore Southern cemeteries on your own.

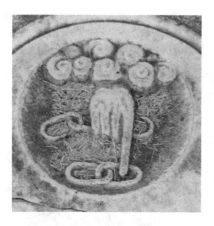

The Hand of God
God reaching down from heaven, plucking links out of a chain, symbolizing members of a family who have died

A Garland or Wreath
Stands for victory over death

Lamb
Stands for innocence, and means that a child is buried in the plot

Urn
An urn stands for immortality. If it is draped, it indicates mourning

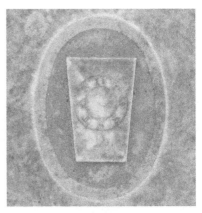

Clasped Hands
The good-byes said at death.
If one hand is masculine and
the other feminine, it
indicates a husband and wife
meeting once again after
death

Masonic Keystone
Grave of a Royal Arch
Mason (of the York Rite
Masons) – the letters
"HTWSSTKS," mean
"Hiram the Widow's Son
Sent to King Solomon"

Crown
Indicates the glory of
life after death

Heavenly Gates
The entrance of the
deceased into heaven

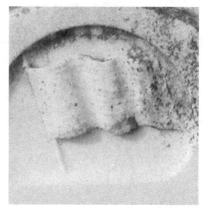

Flower
The fragility of life – this
may further be illustrated by
a broken stem on the flower

Flag
Indicates patriotism or love
for country; especially on the
headstone of a veteran

Dove in Flight
Illustrates the flight of
the soul to heaven

Weeping Willow Tree
A symbol of
mourning; grief;
perpetual lament

Hand Pointing Upward
Pointing the way to heaven,
and therefore
the soul's reward

Square and Compass
Masonic symbol; person
buried here was
a member of
the Masonic Lodge

Knights Of Pythias
F, C, B stands for friendship,
charity, and benevolence; a
member of the order is
buried in the plot

Cherub
Indicates the death of an
infant or a child

Woodmen of the World
A symbol showing that the deceased was a member of the fraternal order "Woodmen of the World"

Jesus
Can be Jesus rising, in heaven, or on the cross. All indicate the salvation promised by the Lord

Bible
Stands for a devotion to God; may also be on the headstone of a pastor or church teacher

Ship
Illustrates passage to the other side; often found on the grave of a sailor

Winged Skull
Death, mortality,
and the ascension
into heaven

Wheat
Represents the harvest being
over; usually found on
graves of the elderly

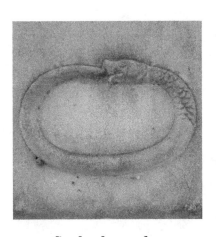

Snake, hooped
A symbol of eternal life;
no ending, no beginning

XP, overlapped
The Chi-Rho, one of the
oldest Christian symbols; XP
are the first two letters of the
Greek word for Christ

Weeping Woman
Grief, mourning; usually
found on the grave of a
departed husband

IHS
Often overlapped, IHS are
the first three letters of Jesus
written in Greek

Shoes
Indicate the death of a child;
often one is overturned

Figure in Shell
Symbolizes rebirth
through baptism

Hourglass
Stands for the passage of
time; wings indicate how fast
time flies by

Owl
Indicates wisdom or
vigilance in life

Grapes
Symbolizes the blood of
Christ, shed for redemption

Anchor
Stands for hope or eternal
life; can also indicate the
grave of a sailor

Menorah
The person buried in the grave is Jewish

Inverted Torch
The inverted torch indicates death, but the flame is for continuing life

Charity Box
Shows that the deceased was a generous and charitable person in life

Sacred Heart
A Catholic symbol that stands for the suffering of Christ

Child
Indicates that an infant or
child is buried there

Draped Headstone
Indicates mourning for the
deceased

Broken Wheel
Symbolizes death; the break
in the circle of life

Butterfly
Stands for the
metamorphosis of the
person from human
to spirit

Funerals and Grieving Today

Some of the funeral and mourning practices of the Old South probably seem bizarre to us today. While there are a few things that have survived, such as pallbearers and placing flowers on the door, how strange it would be in our world to call the local sin eater when someone died, or rent a grave gun to foil the terrible Resurrection Men, or even print funeral tickets for prospective attendees. Yet, these things were all very common in the Old South.

We have new customs, that seem normal to us today but have only surfaced in the last decade or so. It may be that one day they are as strange to a future generation as a Coffin Torpedo is to us. Here are but a few…

The Funeral Program

This is basically the modern day version of the funeral biscuit. If you recall from that particular chapter, at the end of the service, a young man and young woman would stand on either side of the exit door and hand out the cookies, which were wrapped in paper with information about the deceased, a poem or Bible verse, and any other information that the family wanted to include.

In our world, these have been replaced by the simple funeral program that contains much of the same information, including a photograph of the deceased.

They are simple, easy to produce, and don't require any baking at all.

Funeral Food

Today in Southern culture, food is still very much a part of funerals, but for much more practical reasons. When friends learn of a death, the first order of business is to prepare a dish and take it to the family of the deceased: fried chicken, cornbread, creamed potatoes, green bean casserole, or any number of other Southern standards.

This bit of hospitality is done to relieve the family of the duty of having to cook as relatives are arriving from out of town and the family gathers to mourn. An after-funeral meal is then organized by the church or other organization to which the deceased belonged, and it is normally restricted to the family members to give them an opportunity to fellowship together before they depart for their homes.

ngeles Fire Department in
California for many years.
In lieu of flowers, please
make a donation to the First
Cumberland Presbyterian
Church at 2401 Alpine Rd

Flowers or Donations "In Lieu of"

Everyone has seen requests like this; they've become very commonplace... "In lieu of flowers, please make a donation to [insert the family's favorite charity here]."

This is an evolution from the early days. Originally there was a necessity of having flowers at a funeral to help maintain a pleasant aroma there, and then flowers became a Southern tradition as a show of condolence and respect. In our world today, though, people have begun to realize that the money for flowers could be directed into more productive avenues.

A floral arrangement might be anywhere from seventy-five to two hundred dollars or more, and often the family realizes that the flowers would be discarded after the funeral. A donation to a charity in the name of the deceased could go on doing good for a long time, so this type of request is becoming more and more common. Usually the named charity is a favorite of the person who died, or is a group working to address whatever disease or condition took the deceased's life.

Pallbearers and Honorary Pallbearers

The idea of pallbearers has not changed all that much in Southern tradition. Today, most funeral homes have small trolleys for the casket to rest on that allows it to be rolled from one location to the next in the course of the funeral, so the duty of actually carrying it for long distances has diminished considerably. Pallbearers wearing boutonnieres only load the casket into the hearse, and then unload it to the gravesite.

Some families also appoint honorary pallbearers, which is a title of respect, but does not require any physical effort on the person's part. This is done when there are people who the family feels should be recognized as pallbearers, but they are not able to participate in lifting or carrying the coffin.

Memorial Slide Show

This is a staple at most every Southern funeral that you attend today – it is basically a slide show with scenes from the departed one's life. It is usually played before the funeral as the guests are being seated and is often accompanied by a warm, light soundtrack.

Families include many different things, but the funeral directors usually encourage them to submit photographs from different ages of the departed's life, including pictures of him with family members and friends. It is put together by the funeral home and is truly a tribute to that person's life.

After the service, the funeral home presents a video recording of the memorial slide show to the family of the deceased as a memory of their loved one.

Grave Decorations

Cemeteries have mixed emotions about this new trend of using grave decorations. Of course, flowers have been placed at headstones for all of memorable history. Lately, however, families have taken to adding everything from flags, solar-powered lights, stuffed animals, and well, you name it.

This can make the cemeteries hard to mow and maintain, so many have established strict rules about what can and cannot be placed on a grave. Others give the families a wide berth, and allow them to place things that help them with the grieving process.

Roadside Memorials

Everyone has seen these roadside memorials that crop up after a deadly automobile accident.

Some are very discreet, while others are quite elaborate. Southern states are struggling with how to deal with these – on one hand, it is not only a chance to let a family grieve, but is also a reminder to drivers that automobiles must be operated in a safe manner or the results can be tragic. On the other hand, the state transportation departments are hesitant to have colorful distractions placed along the roadside.

Currently, most states allow the roadside memorials, although a few have adopted pre-designed signs that can be purchased by a family that have a generic message such as, "Drive Safely in Memory of Jane Doe."

Drive-Thru Viewing

Believe it or not, the drive-thru concept has expanded to the funeral industry in the last few years. We've seen drive-thru fast food, drive-thru banking, drive-thru pharmacies, but now the world of convenience has been taken to a new level... drive-thru body viewing.

A number of funeral homes have put in a drive-thru lane that allows mourners to simply drive through, pay their last respects to the departed, and then continue on about their day.

There's no question that this is convenient, but you have to admit, it doesn't seem as respectful as walking into the funeral home, signing the guest book, and giving the grieving family a hug. But in today's hectic world, it's really no surprise that it's being offered to mourners even though it flies in the face of Southern hospitality.

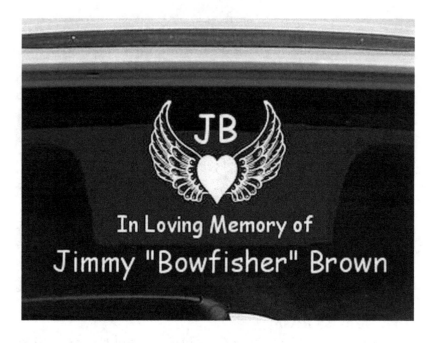

Rear Window Memorials

Who hasn't seen one of these memorial messages emblazoned across the back window of a car or pickup truck while driving down the road or in a McDonald's parking lot?

The rear window memorials seem to be everywhere, and there are websites that will not only let the grieving family member or friend personalize the memorial with just a few keystrokes, and will deliver the decal in very short order.

Much like the mourning clothes of the Old South, this is a way to show the public that someone dear has been lost, and the person whose car has the memorial is mourning them. Not that far a leap from mourning clothes, actually.

Thumbprint Memorial Jewelry

One of the most popular items available today for a mourning family is a piece of jewelry created from the thumbprint of the deceased. There are many different styles available, from pins to pennants to key rings, and the selection continues to grow with the popularity.

In one interview, a businessperson from a funeral home stated that the thumbprint jewelry had become a mainstay of their business, and was in fact one of their best selling memorial items.

Widows frequently wear their husband's thumbprint on a chain as a pennant, along with other items such as his wedding ring.

Coins on the Grave

The leaving of mementos on the final resting places of people dates back to the beginning of time – not just in the Old South, but around the world.

Excavations of even the earliest graves uncover goods meant to serve the deceased in the next world, such as pottery, weapons and beads. The earliest known coins that have been left at a grave date to the late seventh century B.C. As societies began embracing monetary systems, coins began being left in the graves of its citizens merely as yet another way of equipping the dear departed in the afterlife.

In these modern days, coins and other small items are sometimes seen on grave markers, left by visitors for no greater purpose than to indicate that someone has visited that particular grave to pay their respects.

In Closing...

After looking at the funeral and mourning traditions of the Old South, and then paying a quick visit to some of our new ones in the modern day, who is to say which are the more peculiar?

And who knows what changes will come to the funeral industry in the future? Live streaming of memorial services on the Internet, perhaps? Only time will tell.

There can be no doubt, however, that the people of the Old South did what they could to deal with the pain of losing a loved one with the same fervor that we do today – they simply had different customs.

Thankfully we no longer have to worry about watching a coffin alarm to see if a loved one has awoken in the grave, or set traps to foil the dreaded Resurrection Men, or employ the services of the local Sin Eater.

By the same token, imagine the proper Southern family who was at home waiting for a funeral invitation to be told that they could simply hitch up the horse and buggy, and pay their respects to the departed by driving by a plate glass window to view his remains.

Both the society of the Old South and the folks in our own world today struggle to find ways to deal with death and grief. These practices have changed over the years, and will continue to do so. To paraphrase the American philosopher William Ernest Hocking, "Man is the only animal who is able to contemplate his own mortality." As we think of our own death, it makes it all the more important to honor those who have gone on before us.

Index

CPSIA information can be obtained
at www.ICGtesting.com
Printed in the USA
JSHW010045100919
1408JS00007B/22